NAME: _____

A is for Ant

ONE 1

One Frog

Trace the numbers

1

1

1

Write the number 1

My First Practice Activity Book

by

Brynda Dunbar

Title: My First Pratice Activity Book

ISBN 9798322058069

Copyright © 2024 Brynda Dunbar

Thank You

I am Brynda Dunbar and I am a coloring book artist. I create Coloring Books for all ages. My works have been used for Preschool children, Adults and an 80 woman with dementia.

Coloring has been known to induce Stress Relief and Relaxation.

Scan the QR Code below and it will take you to my Amazon Author Page where you can view all the current books that are available. i frequently add new content. If you like what you see, please follow me and this will let you know what are the latest items.

Thank you for taking the time to explore the wonderful world or coloring.

SCAN ME

Brynda Dunbar

This page is for testing out media that you will be using in this book. I am placing a dark blank page after each design to assist with bleeding. If you want to make sure that there is no bleed thru, I would suggest that you place a piece of paper or cardstock behind the page to help prevent bleed thru.

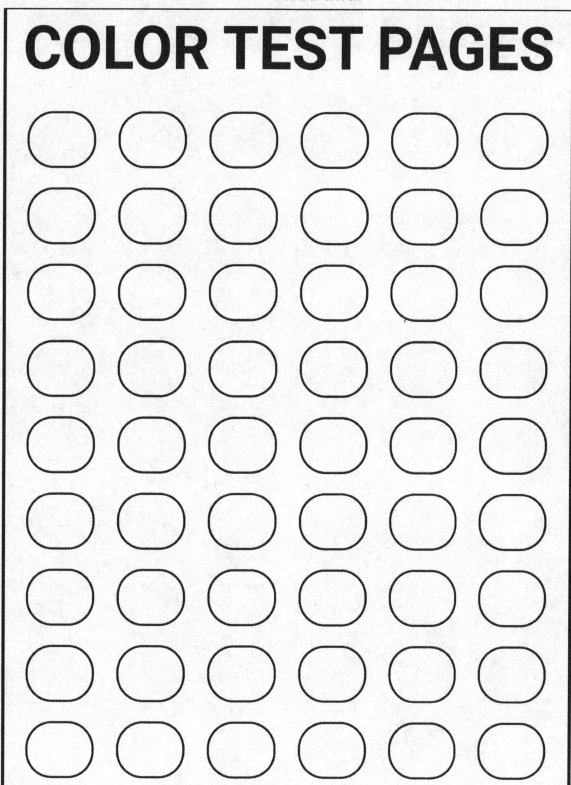

COLOR TEST PAGES

A is for Ant

NAME: _____

A

Color it

A

Trace it

● Trace three words

ANT AXE APPLE

● Write three words, those started Letter: A

NAME: _____

B is for Bee

NAME: _____

B

Color it

B

Trace it

● Trace three words

BEE   BIKE   BIN

● Write three words, those started Letter: B

C is for Cat

NAME: _____

C c

Color it   Trace it

● Trace three words

CAT CAKE COW

● Write three words, those started Letter: C

NAME: _____

D is for Dinosaur

NAME: _____

D

Color it

D

Trace it

● Trace three words

DUCK   DOG   Doll

● Write three words, those started Letter: D

E is for Eye

NAME: _____

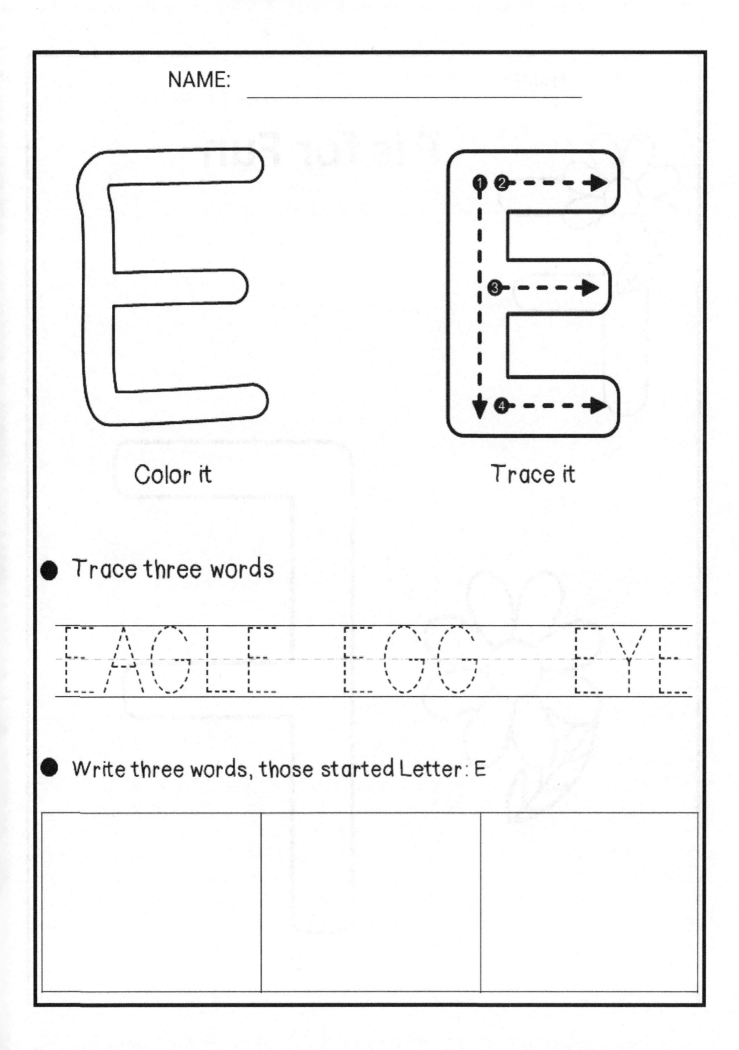

Color it

Trace it

● Trace three words

EAGLE EGG EYE

● Write three words, those started Letter: E

NAME: _____

F is for Fun

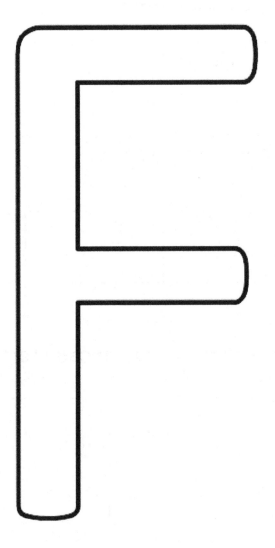

F

F

Color it

Trace it

● Trace three words

FIN   FROG   FUN

● Write three words, those started Letter: F

NAME: _____

G is for Gum

NAME: _____

Color it   Trace it

● Trace three words

GIRL GUN GUM

● Write three words, those started Letter: G

NAME: _____

H is for Hat

H

Color it

Trace it

● Trace three words

HUT   HAT   HOT

● Write three words, those started Letter: H

NAME: _____

I is for Ink

Color it

Trace it

● Trace three words

INK   ICE   IGLOO

● Write three words, those started Letter: I

J is for Jam

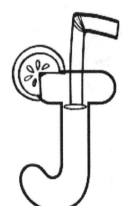

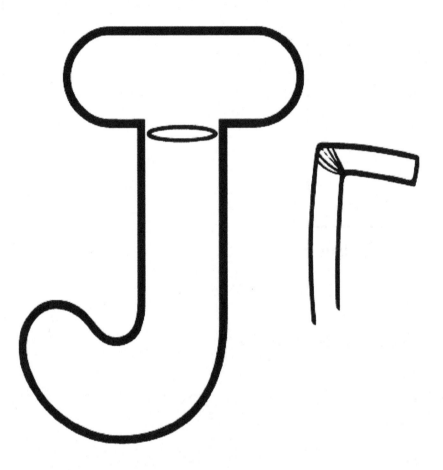

J

Color it

J

Trace it

● Trace three words

JUG   JAM   JEEP

● Write three words, those started Letter: J

NAME: _____

K is for Kid

K

K

Color it

Trace it

● Trace three words

KEY KITE KID

● Write three words, those started Letter: K

Name:_____

L is for Lion

NAME: _____

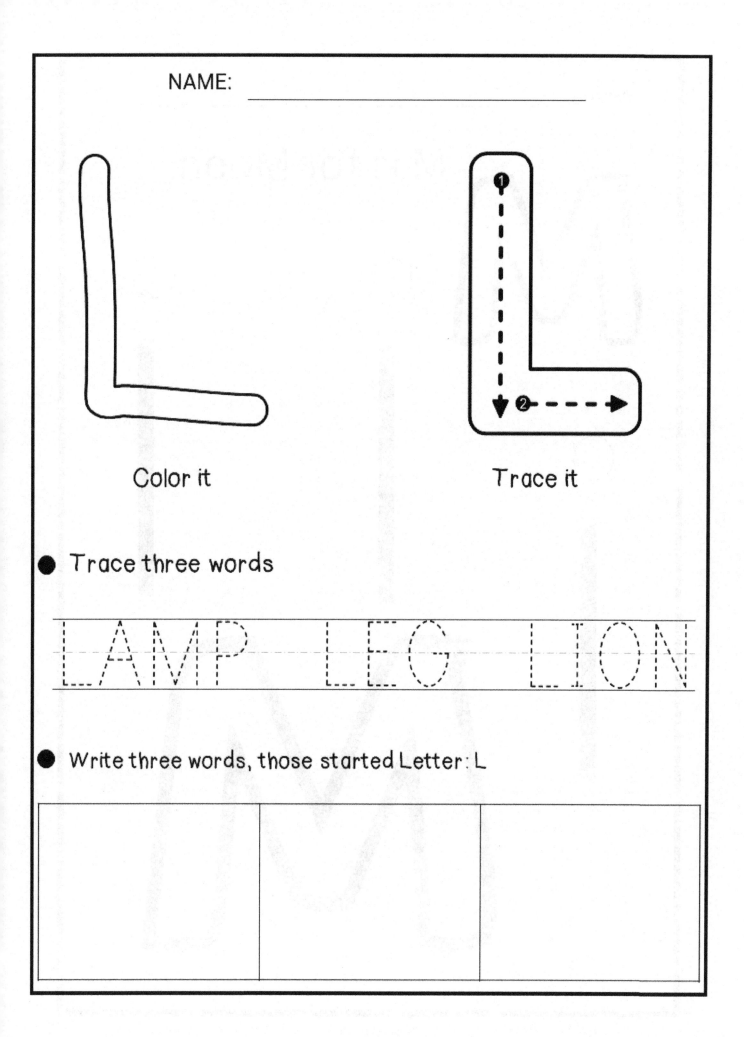

Color it

Trace it

● Trace three words

LAMP LEG LION

● Write three words, those started Letter: L

Name:_____

M is for Moon

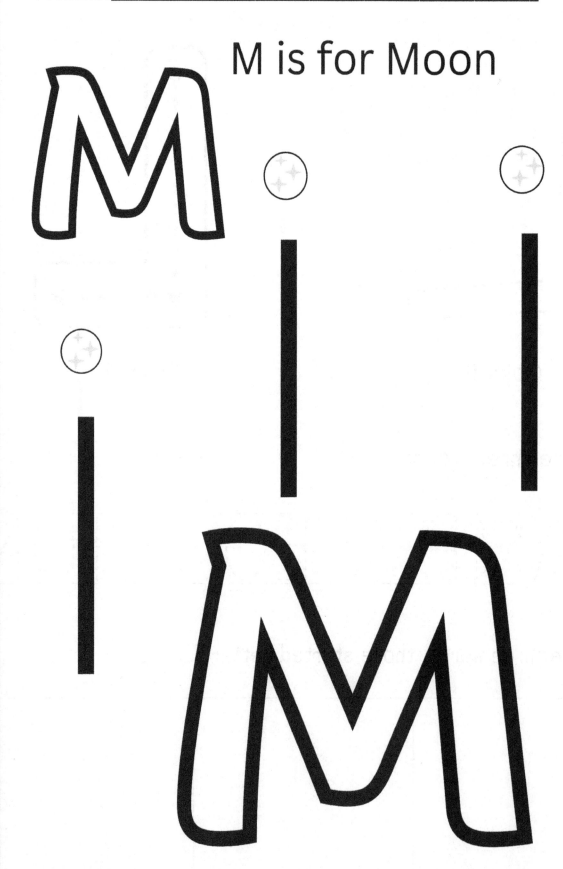

NAME: _____

M

Color it

M

Trace it

● Trace three words

MAP MOON MAD

● Write three words, those started Letter: M

N is for Nap

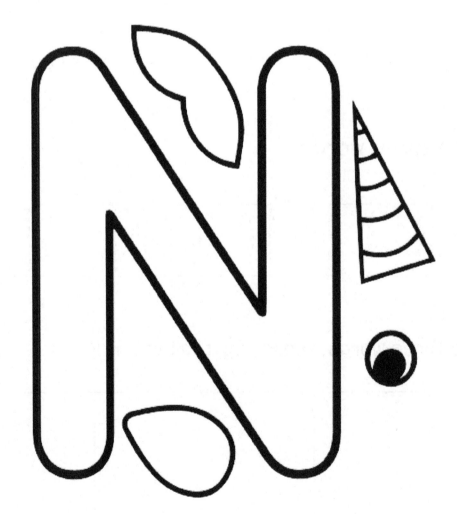

N

Color it

Trace it

● Trace three words

NAP   NUN   NEST

● Write three words, those started Letter: N

O is for Owl

Color it

Trace it

● Trace three words

OIL   OWL   OVAL

● Write three words, those started Letter: O

NAME: _____

P is for Pig

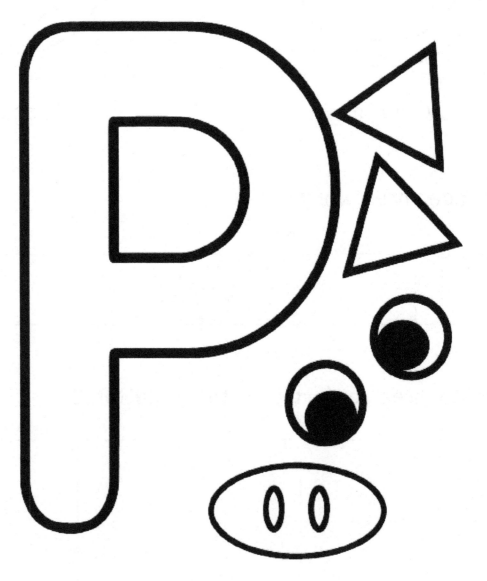

NAME: _____

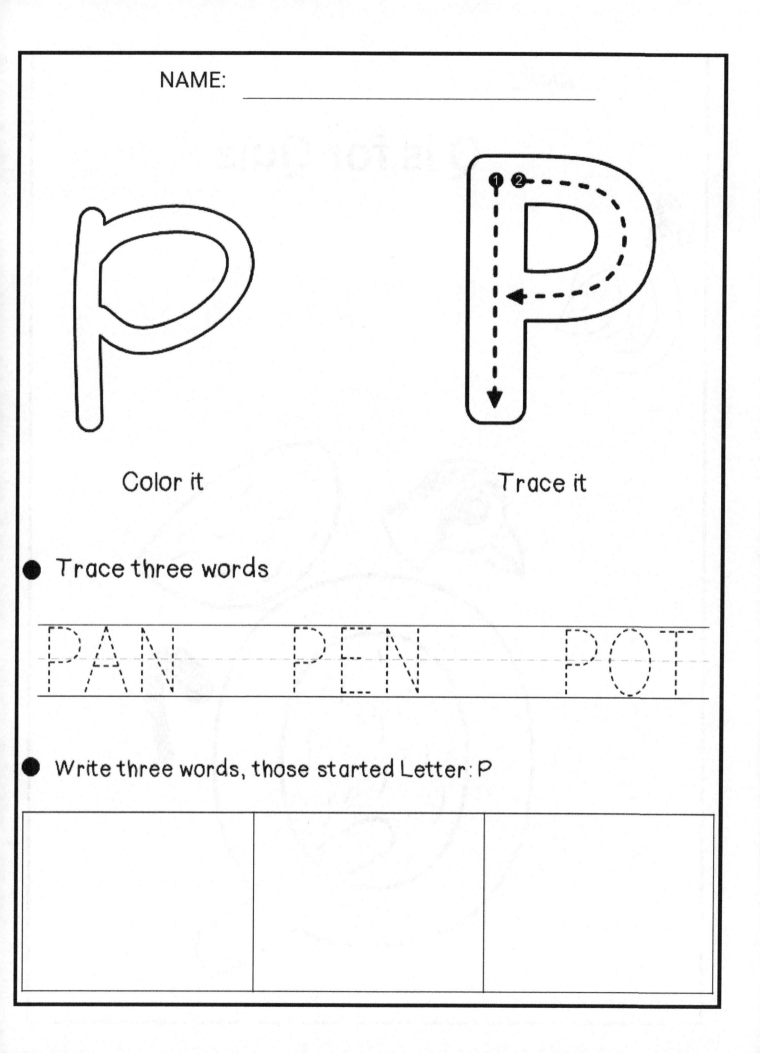

Color it

Trace it

- Trace three words

PAN   PEN   POT

- Write three words, those started Letter: P

NAME: _____

Q is for Quiz

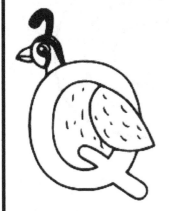

NAME: _____

Color it   Trace it

● Trace three words

QUILT   QUIZ   QUEEN

● Write three words, those started Letter: Q

NAME: _____

R is for Ring

NAME: _____

R

Color it

R

Trace it

● Trace three words

RAT   RING   ROSE

● Write three words, those started Letter: R

S is for Star

S   S

Color it   Trace it

● Trace three words

SUN   STAR   SHIP

● Write three words, those started Letter: R

NAME: _____

T is for Tree

T

Color it

T

Trace it

● Trace three words

TREE   TOP   TOB

● Write three words, those started Letter: T

U is for Uncle

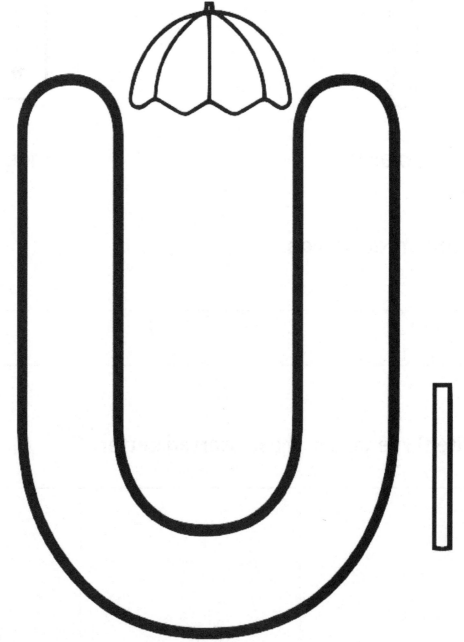

NAME: _____

U

Color it

U

Trace it

● Trace three words

UNCLE   UNDER   UGLY

● Write three words, those started Letter: U

V is for Van

NAME: _____

V

Color it

V

Trace it

● Trace three words

VAN   VASE   VEST

● Write three words, those started Letter: V

NAME: _____

W is for Worm

NAME: _____

W

W

Color it

Trace it

● Trace three words

WALL   WOOL   WHAT

● Write three words, those started Letter: W

Name:_____

X is for X-Ray

NAME: _____

X   X

Color it   Trace it

● Trace three words

X-MASS X-RAY XERUS

● Write three words, those started Letter: X

Y is for Yak

Y Y

Color it

Trace it

● Trace three words

YALK   YOYO   YARN

● Write three words, those started Letter : Y

Z is for Zebra

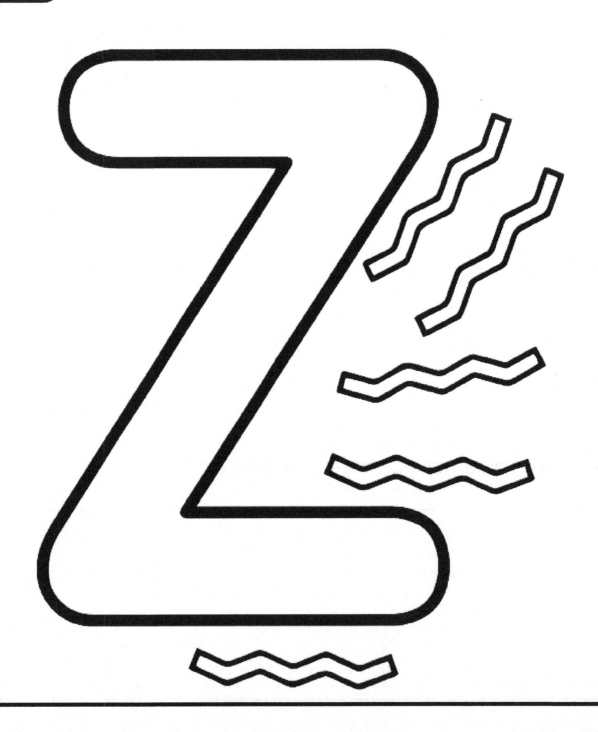

NAME: _____

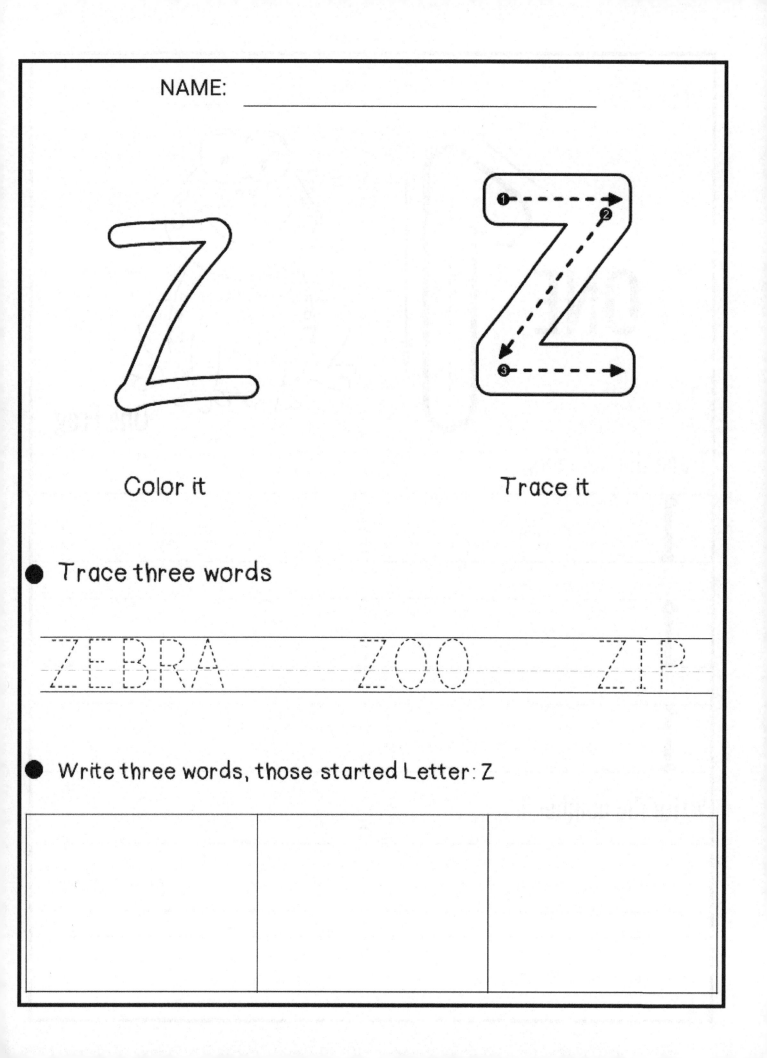

Color it

Trace it

● Trace three words

ZEBRA   ZOO   ZIP

● Write three words, those started Letter: Z

ONE **1**

One Frog

Trace the numbers

1

1

1

Write the number 1

TWO 2

Two Sword

Trace the numbers

2 _2 _2 _2 _2 _2

2 _2 _2 _2 _2 _2

2 _2 _2 _2 _2 _2

Write the number 2

Name:_____

THREE 3

Three Hen

Trace the numbers

3 3 3 3 3 3

3 3 3 3 3 3

3 3 3 3 3 3

Write the number 3

Name:————————————————————

FOUR 4

Four Pencil

Trace the numbers

4

4

4

Write the number 4

Five **5**

Five Elephant

Trace the numbers

5   5   5   5   5   5

5   5   5   5   5   5

5   5   5   5   5   5

Write the number 5

Name:_____

Six

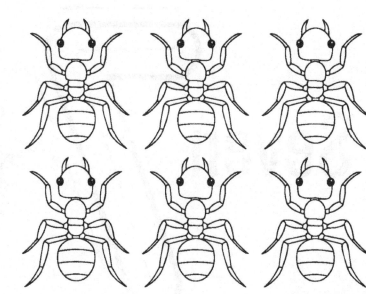

Six Ant

Trace the numbers

6   6   6   6   6   6   6

6   6   6   6   6   6   6

6   6   6   6   6   6   6

Write the number 6

Name: _____

Seven 7

Seven Bird

Trace the numbers

7 / / / / / / / / / /

7 / / / / / / / / / /

7 / / / / / / / / / /

Write the number 7

Eight **8**

Eight Moon

Trace the numbers

8 8 8 8 8 8 8

8 8 8 8 8 8 8

8 8 8 8 8 8 8

Write the number 8

Nine **9**

Nine Star

Trace the numbers

9   9   9   9   9   9   9

9   9   9   9   9   9   9

9   9   9   9   9   9   9

Write the number 9

Name:——————————————————

Ten

10

Ten Football

Trace the numbers

10 10 10 10 10 10 10

10 10 10 10 10 10 10

10 10 10 10 10 10 10

Write the number 10

Congratulations
Good job

NAME:

You have completed this book with new skills!!!!!!

KEEP UP THE GOOD WORK

Thank You

Thank you for your purchase! If you have enjoyed this book, please consider dropping us a review. It takes 5 seconds and helps small businesses like ours.

The QR Code below will take you to your purchase.

Made in the USA
Las Vegas, NV
02 December 2024

13185609R00046